CITY OF COUGHING
AND DEAD RADIATORS

OTHER BOOKS BY MARTÍN ESPADA

POETRY

Rebellion Is the Circle of a Lover's Hands

Trumpets from the Islands of Their Eviction

The Immigrant Iceboy's Bolero

TRANSLATION

The Blood That Keeps Singing:
Selected Poems of Clemente Soto Vélez
(with Camilo Pérez-Bustillo)

CITY OF

COUGHING

AND DEAD

RADIATORS

POEMS

MARTÍN ESPADA

W. W. NORTON & COMPANY

NEW YORK   LONDON

Copyright © 1993 by Martín Espada

Printed in the United States of America

First Edition

The text of this book is composed in 12 on 14.5 Bodoni Book,
with the display set in Bodoni Bold Italic.
Composition by PennSet, Inc.
Manufacturing by The Courier Companies, Inc.
Book design by Margaret M. Wagner.

Library of Congress Cataloging-in-Publication Data
Espada, Martín, 1957–
City of coughing and dead radiators : poems / Martín Espada.
p.   cm.
1. Puerto Ricans—United States—Poetry.   1. Title.
PS3555.S53C57   1993
811'.54—dc20   93-9911

ISBN 0-393-03555-7

W. W. Norton & Company, Inc., 500 Fifth Avenue, New York, N.Y. 10110
W. W. Norton & Company Ltd., 10 Coptic Street, London WC1A 1PU

1 2 3 4 5 6 7 8 9 0

Contents

I

Cockroaches of Liberation

The Hidalgo's Hat and a Hawk's Bell of Gold   17

The Admiral and the Snake   19

The Lover of a Subversive
  Is Also a Subversive   21

Cockroaches of Liberation   23

El Grito de Pepaberta   25

Coca-Cola and Coco Frío   26

Day of the Dead on Wortman Avenue   28

Borofels   30

Prayer for Brother Burglar   32

The Skull Beneath the Skin of the Mango   34

Fidel in Ohio   36

II

CITY OF COUGHING AND DEAD RADIATORS

City of Coughing and Dead Radiators 39

Courthouse Graffiti for Two Voices 42

Tires Stacked in the Hallways
   of Civilization 43

Mi Vida: Wings of Fright 44

The Broken Window of Rosa Ramos 46

The Legal Aid Lawyer Has an Epiphany 48

Who Burns for the Perfection of Paper 49

The Toolmaker Unemployed 50

Transient Hotel Sky at the Hour of Sleep 52

The Music of Astronomy 55

Don't Worry, Son, You're in the Care
   of Mental Health Professionals 56

The Arm 57

Memorial Day Parade
   at the Viet Coffee House 58

Ashes and Donuts 59

DSS Dream 60

III

WHEN SONGS BECOME WATER

Blackballed by the Rainbow Girls   63

White Birch   66

The Carnival Leaves for the Next Town   68

The Rifle in My Hands   69

The Lesson of My Uncle's Nose   70

The Year I Was Diagnosed
   with a Sacrilegious Heart   72

The Other Alamo   75

Author's Note: When Songs Become Water   79

When Songs Become Water   80

Cuando los cantos se vuelven agua   81

Glossary of Spanish Terms   85

Biographical Note   89

ACKNOWLEDGMENTS

Some of these poems have appeared in the following publications:

Boston Review (vol. XVII, no. 4, September/October 1992): "The Hidalgo's Hat and a Hawk's Bell of Gold."

Callaloo (vol. 15, no. 4, Fall 1992): "The Broken Window of Rosa Ramos."

Denver Quarterly (vol. 27, no. 1, Summer 1992): "Cockroaches of Liberation"; "The Toolmaker Unemployed"; "The Year I Was Diagnosed with a Sacrilegious Heart."

Diario Latino (February 8, 1992): "Cuando los cantos se vuelven agua."

Kenyon Review (vol. XIII, no. 4, Fall 1991, and vol. XV, no. 1, Winter 1993): "City of Coughing and Dead Radiators"; "Mi Vida."

Painted Bride Quarterly (no. 48, 1992): "When Songs Become Water"; "Cuando los cantos se vuelven agua."

Ploughshares (vol. 17, no. 4, Winter 1991–92, and vol. 19, no. 1, Spring 1993): "The Other Alamo"; "Who Burns for the Perfection of Paper."

Review: Latin American Literature and Arts (no. 45, July December 1991): "The Admiral and the Snake"; "Borofels"; "El Grito de Pepaberta"; "The Rifle in My Hands"; "When Songs Become Water." Copyright *Review;* reprinted by permission.

Many thanks to Jack Agüeros, Alicia Borinsky, Camilo Pérez-Bustillo, Cyrus Cassells, Josh Cohen, Carolyn Forché, Cola Franzen, Luis Garden, Alan Gilbert, Roberto Márquez, Marilyn Hacker, Lawrence Joseph, Dan Shapiro, Earl Shorris, Gary Soto, Joseph Spieler, and Clemente Soto Vélez for their support of this work.

I

COCKROACHES

OF

LIBERATION

THE HIDALGO'S HAT
AND A HAWK'S BELL OF GOLD

Columbus hallucinated gold
wherever sunlight darted
from rock to water, spelled the word
slowly in his logbook
so that the Lord might see
and blow his ship
into a storm of gleaming dust.
When God would not puff his cheeks
for trade winds of gold, the Admiral flourished
a decree on parchment: a hawk's bell
full of gold from every Indio
where the rivers gilded the soil
of Española, 1495.

The Indios could only load the bells
with mirrored sunlight. For bells
without gold, the hands were pressed together
as if in prayer, gripped on the block,
then the knobs of wrists were splintered
by a bright and heavy sword.
Their stumps became torches
seething flames of blood,
the vowels of their language
lamentations flattening the tongue.

While the Admiral slept
in the exhaustion of dysentery,

or amused the Queen
with his zoo of shackled caciques,
the town he named Isabela
dissolved into the stones
like a rumor of gold, deserted swampground.
There is a spirit legend:
that the moans of men in rusting helmets
would radiate from the vine-matted walls,
starved with a mouthful of bark
or mad with a brain soaking in syphilis,
or digging an arrowhead from the eye
fired by an Indio with two hands.

Someone saw the hidalgos there, ghosts of noblemen
bowing in a row, a swirl of velvet cloaks.
As each swept off his feathered hat
in greeting, his head unscrewed
from the hollow between caped shoulders,
swinging in the hat
like a cannonball in a sack.

—*C ULEBRA , P UERTO R ICO, 1990*

On the island of the snake,
a man with one ear
sells canned sausage at the bodega
fingerprinted in dust.

Blustering Navy gunboats
dubbed the town Dewey for the admiral,
then splintered the vertebrae of the coral reef
with years of blast-intoxicated target practice,
and still no one can walk.
Nets hauled brass shells
in the dripping absence of fish,
so fishermen swept dirt by day,
redundant as scratching roosters.
Despite the wild incandescent missiles
dimming into the glow of the wake,
and jailhouse suffocation
for those who leaped the barbed wire
stitching the beach,
the trespassers and saboteurs returned
like a resurrection of mosquitoes, till the commanders
canceled the rehearsal for apocalypse at last.

After the shelling no longer
spat the sand in thunderous geysers,
came the whistling artillery of the hurricane.
Past the trees decapitated

and the shacks collapsed
by a storm kicking
at the toys that tripped her,
two abandoned tanks like hollow iron crabs
crumble in webs and flakes of rust
on the beach, sunburned sentries
marooned after the looting, gun barrels
saluting the bay where ships
with plunder in the belly
stirred a white foam,
monuments to a riot of sailors
and obscene songs about the admiral.

The lover of a subversive
is also a subversive.
The painter's compañero was a conspirator,
revolutionary convicted
to haunt the catacombs of federal prison
for the next half century.
When she painted her canvas
on the beach, the FBI man
squatted behind her
on the sand, muddying his dark gray suit
and kissing his walkie-talkie,
a pallbearer who missed
the funeral train.

The painter who paints a subversive
is also a subversive.
In her portrait of him, she imagines
his long black twist of hair. In her portraits
of herself, she wears a mask
or has no mouth. She must sell the canvases,
for the FBI man ministered solemnly
to the principal at the school
where she once taught.

The woman who grieves for a subversive
is also a subversive.
The FBI man is a pale-skinned apparition

staring in the subway.
She could reach for him
and only touch a pillar of ash
where the dark gray suit had been.
If she hungers to touch her lover,
she must brush her fingers
on moist canvas.

The lover of a subversive
is also a subversive.
When the beach chilled cold,
and the bright stumble of tourists
deserted, she and the FBI man
were left alone with their spying glances,
as he waited calmly
for the sobbing to begin,
and she refused to sob.

COCKROACHES OF LIBERATION

—FOR VÍCTOR RIVERA, PUERTO RICO

Near the campus, every night,
there was a ceremony
familiar and savored
as piragua, fruit syrup on ice:
First, the student strike,
congregating on the plaza
with songs taunting
the governor and the chancellor
in rhyme, five beats of the clave,
placards accusing collaboration
with bankers and the Marines.

Then, every night,
the canter of the police,
rumbling on cobblestone
through the plaza
in the wake of dropped leaflets,
clubs sweeping at heads
like cop fantasies
of Roberto Clemente at bat,
though his spirit spat back
the water that drowned him
in shame.

Everyone had a spell for disappearing,
a secret for dissolving
between the grillwork of balconies

and fire escapes, down hallways
with a single dead bulb, basement steps.
The plaza was an empty postcard.

Later, after the flashlights
and battery-charged eyes of the cops
had dimmed,
they crept back onto the plaza,
calling to each other
with the wooden clap of the claves
and hands slapping time till
the beat bounced off cobblestone,
feasting on rebel songs
cool on the tongue
as fruit syrup and ice,
multiplying in the dark
like cockroaches of liberation
too quick for stomping boots
that circle back on the hour,
immune to the stink
of government fumigation.

—U TUADO, P UERTO R ICO

A hundred years ago,
on coquí frog-chanting nights,
ancestor Pepaberta
would lift the oil lamp
and stuff a pistol
in her waist
for travels to the outhouse
leaning between the hills,
dueling with rodent viceroys
and their insect infantry
and no one asked
who else.

The shots
spooked the roosters
that hollered in the dark,
woke men muttering
about the loca
who kept their bladders full
till morning.

On his first visit to Puerto Rico,
island of family folklore,
the fat boy wandered
from table to table
with his mouth open.
At every table, some great-aunt
would steer him with cool spotted hands
to a glass of Coca-Cola.
One even sang to him, in all the English
she could remember, a Coca-Cola jingle
from the forties. He drank obediently, though
he was bored with this potion, familiar
from soda fountains in Brooklyn.

Then, at a roadside stand off the beach, the fat boy
opened his mouth to coco frío, a coconut
chilled, then scalped by a machete
so that a straw could inhale the clear milk.
The boy tilted the green shell overhead
and drooled coconut milk down his chin;
suddenly, Puerto Rico was not Coca-Cola
or Brooklyn, and neither was he.

For years afterward, the boy marveled at an island
where the people drank Coca-Cola
and sang jingles from World War II
in a language they did not speak,
while so many coconuts in the trees
sagged heavy with milk, swollen
and unsuckled.

Halloween in Brooklyn:
wearing the baggy costumes
of monsters, we were not allowed
to fill our bags
outside the sullen brick building
where we lived,
because, the voices said,
real monsters peered
between the slats of benches
in the projects.
One shot the grocer, and the witness,
a woman who worshiped a dry God,
needed rum for the first time.

At 245 Wortman Avenue,
bedsheet ghosts pounded doors
that opened on a leash of chain,
then banged shut to shield hermits
with white hair and burglarized faces,
stunned at night by the slapped-mouth madrigal
of a woman somewhere in the building.

From doorways suspicious hands
lifted the masks of comic book heroes
to avoid feeding the same hero twice,
index fingers lecturing on gratitude
to children who pissed

in a malicious shower
from 10th-floor terraces
of concrete and chicken wire
on other nights.

Drunk on chocolate,
shoving and bickering,
we sorted the bags by night's end,
wary of pins and razors,
trashing unwrapped possible poison
in the hallway incinerator,
crematorium of dead cats.

So the Day of the Dead
was celebrated on Wortman Avenue
with the lust of a paranoid
for the enemy,
beating steam pipes with a broom
for silence overhead,
growling threats at the ceiling.

— FOR SONIA NIETO

In Brooklyn, the mice were crazy
with courage, bony gray pickpockets
snatching crumbs from plates
at the table. The roaches
panicked in spirals on the floor,
or weaved down walls
for the sanctuary of cracked paint.
No heat, so the oven door drooped open
like an immigrant's surprise.

Sonia's mother was mute in English,
mouth chapped and coughing
without words to yell for heat.
But the neighbors spoke of Borofels:
Tell Borofels, and mice shrivel in traps,
roaches kick in poisoned heaps,
steam pipes bang so loud
that windows open in winter.

Sonia and her mother sailed
on a subway train rocking like a ship
desperate for light, then rose
in an untranslated territory
of Brooklyn. So Sonia translated:
"Where is Borofels?"
No one knew; the girl pinballed

by strangers in a hurry, hooded against frost
as mouths puffed quick clouds of denial.

Sonia saw the uniform then,
blue-coated trooper of the U.S. Mail,
and pleaded for Borofels.
His face, drowsing in bewilderment,
awoke with the gust
of what he suddenly understood,
and he pointed down the street:
"You want
the Board of Health."

They could yell now
like banned poets
back from exile.

—FOR DV

He was once the adolescent junkie,
green eyes alert, who could ease
locked bedroom doors aside
and scoop jewelry, cameras, clock radios
awakening no one.

Twenty years grew swirls on his knuckles
and red flags in the hollows of his hands.
A bullhorn man among strikers,
driving for the Solidarity Cab Company,
he called himself a taxista Marxista-Leninista
and told of marching through his history
with the limbs of a dead street rebel
spread-eagled across shoulders,
rifles shaken overhead,
the blackout that follows the billyclub,
each compañero and each cop named
with the witness of a hand
missing one thumb.

Once he clicked off the meter
and quietly coaxing tickled my door open
to prove his weather-brown hands still clever
even missing one thumb,
work boots tramping through the room
like tire tracks on the sidewalk,
hard-bellied man in overalls and a baseball cap

booming the Internationale at me
on the toilet.

Many jobs later, he was fired for words
drilled in the face
of an embezzling boss,
and this after all cash spent
on a racehorse
too old for anyone else to buy.
He draped his heavy horse blankets
on a clothesline in my apartment for two weeks,
then bounced away in a rattling white van.

May his hands still be smart,
may his thumb grow back
to better grip the bullhorn
or the boss's collar.

THE SKULL BENEATH THE
SKIN OF THE MANGO

—El Salvador, 1992

The woman spoke
with the tranquillity of shock:
the Army massacre was here.
But there were no peasant corpses,
no white crosses; even the houses
gone. Cameras chattered,
notebooks filled with rows of words.
Some muttered that slaughter
is only superstition
in a land of new treaties and ballot boxes.

Everyone gathered mangoes
before leaving. An American reporter,
arms crowded with fruit, could not see
what he kicked jutting from the ground.
He glanced down and found his sneaker
pressing against the forehead
of a human skull, yellow
like the flesh of a mango.

He wondered how many skulls
are crated with the mangoes
for sale at market, how many
grow yellow flesh and green skin
in the wooden boxes exported
to the States. This would explain,
he said to me,
why so many bodies
are found without heads
in El Salvador.

The bus driver tore my ticket
and gestured at the tabloid
spread across the steering wheel.
The headline:
FIDEL CASTRO DEAD
REPLACED BY IDENTICAL DOUBLE
Below, two photographs of Fidel,
one with cigar, one without.

"The resemblance is amazing,"
the driver said,
and I agreed.

II

CITY

OF

COUGHING

AND

DEAD

RADIATORS

CITY OF COUGHING
AND DEAD RADIATORS

—CHELSEA, MASSACHUSETTS

I cannot evict them
from my insomniac nights,
tenants in the city of coughing
and dead radiators.
They bang the radiators
like cold hollow marimbas;
they cry out
to unseen creatures
skittering across their feet
in darkness;
they fold hands over plates
to protect food
from ceilings black with roaches.

And they answer the call
of the list,
all evictions in court,
brays the clerk.
Quiet and dutiful
as spectral troops returning,
they file into the courtroom,
crowding the gallery:
the patient one from El Salvador,
shoemakers' union refugee,
slapping his neck
to show where that vampire
of an Army bullet

pierced his uncle's windpipe;
the red-haired woman
with no electricity
but the drug's heat
swimming in the pools
of her blue bruises,
white-skinned as the candles
she lives by,
who will move this afternoon
for a hundred dollars;
the prostitute swollen
with pregnancy and sobbing
as the landlady
sneers miscarriage
before a judge
poking his broken hearing aid;
the girl surrounded by a pleading carousel
of children, in Spanish bewilderment,
sleepless and rat-vigilant,
who wins reluctant extermination
but loses the youngest,
lead paint retarded;
the man alcohol-puffed,
graph of scars
stretching across his belly,
locked out, shirt stolen,
arrested at the hearing

for the rampage
of his detox hallucinations;
the Guatemalan boy, who listens
through the wall
for his father's landlord-defiant staccato,
jolted awake
by flashes of the landlord
floating over the bed,
parade balloon
waving a kitchen knife.

For all those sprawled down stairs
with the work boot's crusted map
printed on the back,
the creases of the judge's face
collapse into a fist.
As we shut files
and click briefcases
to leave,
a loud-faced man
trumpets from the gallery:
Death to Legal Aid.

COURTHOUSE GRAFFITI
FOR TWO VOICES

Jimmy C.
Greatest Car Thief Alive
Chelsea '88

Then what
are you doing
here?

Tires Stacked in the Hallways of Civilization

—CHELSEA, MASSACHUSETTS

"Yes, Your Honor, there are rodents,"
said the landlord to the judge,
"but I let the tenant
have a cat. Besides,
he stacks his tires
in the hallway."

The tenant confessed
in stuttering English:
"Yes, Your Honor,
I am from El Salvador,
and I put my tires
in the hallway."

The judge puffed up
his robes
like a black bird
shaking off rain:
"Tires out of the hallway!
You don't live in a jungle
anymore. This
is a civilized country."

So the defendant was ordered
to remove his tires
from the hallways of civilization,
and allowed to keep the cat.

—*CHELSEA, MASSACHUSETTS, 1987*

The refugee's run
across the desert borderlands
carved wings of fright
into his forehead,
growing more crooked
with every eviction notice
in this waterfront city of the north.

He sat in the office for the poor,
daughter burrowed asleep
on one shoulder,
and spoke to the lawyer
with a voice trained obedient
in the darkness of church confessionals
and police barracks, Guatemalan dusk.

The lawyer nodded through papers,
glancing up only when the girl awoke
to spout white vomit on the floor
and her father's shirt.
"Mi vida": My life, he said,
then said again, as he bundled her
to the toilet.

This was how the lawyer,
who, like the fortune-teller,

had a bookshelf of prophecy
but a cabinet empty of cures,
found himself
kneeling on the floor
with a paper towel.

THE BROKEN WINDOW OF ROSA RAMOS

—CHELSEA, MASSACHUSETTS, 1991

Rosa Ramos could spread her palm
at the faucet for hours
without cold water
ever hissing hot,
while the mice darted
like runaway convicts
from a hole in the kitchen floor.

The landlord was a spy,
clicking his key in the door unheard
to haunt the living room,
peeking for the thrill of young skin,
a pasty dead-faced man still hungry.

Her husband was dead.
She knew this
from *El Vocero* newspaper,
the picture of his grinning face
sprayed with the black sauce of blood,
a bullet-feast.
Rosa shows his driver's license,
a widow's identification,
with the laminated plastic
cracking across his eyes,
so that he watches her
through a broken window.

She leaves the office
rehearsing with the lawyer
new words in English
for the landlord:
"Get out. Get out. Get out."

THE LEGAL AID LAWYER
HAS AN EPIPHANY

—CHELSEA, MASSACHUSETTS

When I bounced off the bus for work
at Legal Aid this morning,
I found the spiky halo of a hole
in the front window of the office,
as if some drunk had rammed
the thorn-crowned head of Jesus
through the glass.
I say Jesus because I followed
the red handprints on the brick
and there he was next door,
a bust in the window
of the botánica,
blood in his hair,
his eyes a bewildered blue
cast heavenward, hoping
for an airlift away from here.
The sign on the door
offered a manicure
with every palm reading.

At sixteen, I worked after high school hours
at a printing plant
that manufactured legal pads:
Yellow paper
stacked seven feet high
and leaning
as I slipped cardboard
between the pages,
then brushed red glue
up and down the stack.
No gloves: fingertips required
for the perfection of paper,
smoothing the exact rectangle.
Sluggish by 9 PM, the hands
would slide along suddenly sharp paper,
and gather slits thinner than the crevices
of the skin, hidden.
Then the glue would sting,
hands oozing
till both palms burned
at the punchclock.

Ten years later, in law school,
I knew that every legal pad
was glued with the sting of hidden cuts,
that every open lawbook
was a pair of hands
upturned and burning.

THE TOOLMAKER UNEMPLOYED

—CONNECTICUT RIVER VALLEY, 1992

The toolmaker
is sixty years old,
unemployed
since the letter
from his boss
at the machine shop.

He carries
a cooler of soda
everywhere,
so as not to carry
a flask of whiskey.

During the hours
of his shift,
he is building a barn
with borrowed lumber
or hacking at trees
in the yard.

The family watches
and listens to talk
of a bullet
in the forehead,
maybe for himself,

50

maybe for the man
holding the second mortgage.

Sometimes
he stares down
into his wallet.

TRANSIENT HOTEL SKY
AT THE HOUR OF SLEEP

On the late shift, front desk,
midnight to 8 AM,
we watched the sky through crusted windows,
till the clouds swirled away
like water in the drain
of a steel sink.

In the clouded liquid light
human shapes would harden,
an Army jacket staggering
against the bannister at bartime,
coal-skinned man
drifting through the lobby
moaning to himself
about Mississippi,
a known arsonist
squeezing his head
in the microwave oven
with a giggle.

As we studied the white face
of the clock above the desk,
fluorescent hum of 4 AM,
a cowboy bragged
about buying good boots
for 19 cents from a retarded man,
then swaggered out the door

with a pickaxe
and a treasure map.
The janitor mopped the floor
nostalgic for Vietnam snapshots
confiscated at the airport,
peasant corpses with jaws
lopsided in a song of missing teeth.

Slowly the sky was a comfort,
like the pillow of a patient
sick for decades
and sleeping at last.
At the hour of sleep
a man called Johnson
trotted down the hallway
and leaned out the window,
then again, haunting
the fifth floor
in a staring litany
of gestures, so even
the security guard on rounds
wrote in the logbook for social workers
who never kept a schedule at night.
Johnson leaped
through the greasy pane of sky
at 5 AM,
refused suicide in flight,

and kicking struggled to stand in the air,
but snapped his ankles on the sidewalk
and burst his head on the curb,
scalp flapped open like the lid
on a bucket of red paint.

The newspaper shocked mouths
that day, but the transient hotel sky
drained pale as usual,
and someone pissed in the ashtray
by the desk, then leered
at the jabbering smokers.

Every night
the ex–mental patient,
forgetful of the medicine
that caused him to forget,
would climb to the roof
of the transient hotel
with a flashlight,
waiting for his Martian parents
and their spaceship,
flashlight beam waving
like the baton of a conductor
firm in the faith
that this orchestra
will one night
give him music.

DON'T WORRY, SON,
YOU'RE IN THE CARE
OF MENTAL HEALTH PROFESSIONALS

I am the man
who spends all day
searching
with a flashlight
under the bed
for the shoes
he's already
wearing

T H E   A R M

—*BOSTON, MASSACHUSETTS, 1985*

A man pushing
onto a subway train
gorged with bodies
is blocked out by the doors
squeezing shut,
but for one arm, caught within.

The arm protrudes at first,
a beggar's patience,
waiting for the doors to open.
But the train instead
locks the arm in its teeth
and lopes across the tracks,
the man in a stumbling waltz
dragged along the platform,
as the fingers of the arm grope out
amid a shrieking aviary of commuters.

As the huge throat of tunnel approaches,
the arm slides down between the doors
and disappears, whether from perseverance
or a body crushing into the wall,
whether mutilation by sleepy conductors
startled by the loud thump from behind,
or salvation by the quick fingers of demons
sneering at their own joke,
no one knows.

MEMORIAL DAY PARADE
AT THE VIET COFFEE HOUSE

—*BOSTON, MASSACHUSETTS*

When the Memorial Day parade
rumbled past the Viet Coffee House,
the iron pachyderm tanks,
boys in green-brown camouflage
proud of crewcuts and memorized
steps to the march,
the clumsy bouquet of flags
and the migraine of the drum, drunken boom,
the objects in the Coffee House
did not stop their business:
the record player warped
a love song in French,
the cigarette smoke
kept whirling only to vanish
at the ceiling,
the pans sloppy with noodles
hissed on the stove.

Only the workers stopped moving,
as all their nightmares, fires
glowing in a darkened valley,
swept up together in a tidal blaze,
in the bombing mission
that swoops and roars
but never leaves this sky.

ASHES AND DONUTS

—*FOR JAN HAIGHT*

Discovering a day-old harvest
in the garbage of the donut shop:
circles, hoops, wheels of sugar and bread
that glued fingers, smeared mouths,
dissolved the stone in the stomach
with a hungry cackle
for welfare family scavengers.

Until the manager, spy in short sleeves
and paper hat, decorated
the donut trash one night
with an icing of ashes
from the day's cigarettes.

The bag ripped, a hand teased with ash,
the stone again scraping their ribs,
they slept on the beach that night,
without the romance of tourists.

I dreamed
the Department of Social Services
came to the door and said:
"We understand
you have a baby,
a goat, and a pig living here
in a two-room apartment.
This is illegal.
We have to take the baby away,
unless you eat the goat."

"The pig's OK?" I asked.
"The pig's OK," they said.

III

WHEN

SONGS

BECOME

WATER

—FOR KLGE

The Rainbow Girls, Daughters of the Masons,
baptized and believers
of the Connecticut River Valley,
lilted from the Book of Ritual:
"If in the years to come, you should be
the wife and mother of a home,
let the lessons of the flag be sacred,"
incantation at the altar
where a spotlight blasted the face
of an open Bible, where white gowns
smoothed over the pangs of city abortions,
as rhinestone tiaras pinned down hangovers
and questions like untrained hair.
The one who memorized quickest,
recited loudest, was named
Grand Chaplain, and her family bragged
at the shop.

At the local Assembly,
rumors were passed and gobbled
like a tray of cookies.
The girl who would join today
was stained by the character of her mother;
the choice of a Puerto Rican stepfather
brought small-town grimaces between sips of Coke.
The Eastern Star, Masonic wife
and chaperone, sucked on her teeth

and said no to the nomination.
But the Grand Chaplain saw God
as a shopkeeper in an apron
with her grandfather's face,
and so she called a vote.

Along the linen dais,
before the Pot of Gold,
the ballot box circulated
among the softly hissing conspiracies
of Masonic daughters,
returning to be counted
with a treasure of black marbles,
jewels the darkness of prohibited skin.
The Grand Chaplain cursed the box shut.

Two weeks later, the Grand Cross of Color
Banquet, assembly of assemblies:
an orbit of chandeliers
hovered above the square tassled heads
of Shriners, bankers and insurance men,
as the auditorium swirled goblets
and awaited the invocation.
But the Grand Chaplain could not pray;
the God with her grandfather's face
slammed his apron on the counter.
Her words shook, then stood

with the faith of a heretic,
about a daughter stained
by her dark pariah stepfather,
blackballed by the Rainbow Girls,
Yankee segregation clean and quiet
as the town common in winter.

She felt that stain spreading brightly
across her own cheeks and forehead,
heard the veins behind her ears
and the room's stillness
rush as she abandoned the podium.
She remembers that the car
where she cried was white
with red seat covers;
her damp face
pressed and stuck.
No God of the grandfather's face
handed her a nickel
for the truth.

WHITE BIRCH

—FOR KATHERINE, DECEMBER 28, 1991

Two decades ago rye whiskey
scalded your father's throat,
stinking from the mouth
as he stamped his shoe
in the groove between your hips,
dizzy flailing cartwheel down the stairs.
The tail of your spine split,
became a scraping hook.
For twenty years a fire raced
across the boughs of your bones,
his drunken mouth a movie
flashing with every stabbed gesture.

Now the white room of birth is throbbing:
the numbers palpitating red on the screen of machinery
tentacled to your arm; the oxygen mask wedged
in a wheeze on your face; the numbing medication
injected through the spine.
The boy was snagged on that spiraling bone.
Medical fingers prodded your raw pink center
while you stared at a horizon of water
no one else could see, creatures leaping silver
with tails that slashed the air
like your agonized tongue.

You were born in the river valley,
hard green checkerboard of farms,

a town of white birches
and a churchyard from the workhorse time,
weathered headstones naming women
drained of blood with infants coiled inside
the caging hips, hymns swaying
as if lanterns over the mounded earth.

Then the white birch of your bones,
resilient and yielding, yielded again,
root snapped as the boy spilled out of you
into hands burst open by beckoning
and voices pouring praise like water,
two beings tangled in exhaustion,
blood-painted, but full of breath.

After a generation of burning
the hook unfurled in your body,
the crack in the bone dissolved:
One day you stood, expected again
the branch of nerves
fanning across your back to flame,
and felt only the grace of birches.

THE CARNIVAL LEAVES
FOR THE NEXT TOWN

— *FOR KLGE*

For you, the carnival meant
a blazing wheel of light
flared over a farming town
of faces from the high school yearbook.
So when the carnival
came to the city,
you hooked my elbow and tugged me,
mannequin of civil disobedience,
to the fairgrounds.

There I shot 21 straight baskets,
spin, flip, quarter a throw,
to win a stuffed parrot
that you grabbed
like a childhood without calluses.

Three AM now, as you sleep,
I puzzle at evaporated days
when my fingertips could read
the grain of the ball
like holy Braille,
when I could squeeze a planet
in my sure hands
and flip it through a hoop.

Four dollar an hour bouncer:
another grunting shove
and blast of obscenities,
cheekbone scraped numb,
heart squeezed again
with the narcotic of the fight,
I heard the rifle crack of my fist
against a beer-dizzy skull;

but listening
for the first time
to that rifle in my hands,
I became a soldier on strike,
weapons dropped amid the bullets' sleet,
hands sick and trembling, face pelted
in the flailing storm of the brawl.

Knuckles dark blue lumps
by morning, I quit the bar
and hid my purple heart
in white bandages.

My uncle promised many times
that I would meet José Basora,
welterweight who twenty years before
fought Sugar Ray Robinson to a draw,
and now stood with folded arms
behind a pyramid of cans,
a grocer in the Bronx.

But I never met him. I watched the fights
on television with my uncle
and sampled the bitterness
of his beer can.
Then he made another promise:
not to punch too hard
when we sparred
with boxing gloves
in the living room.

"One rule," he said.
"Never hit me in the nose.
My nose was broken. See?"—
pressing with a finger.
I did not ask how, in jail
for a pack of cigarettes, or on the sidewalk
jabbing accusations at the card table.
But I was fascinated by my uncle's tattoos,

those hieroglyphics burned into his stringy biceps,
so I nodded yes.

The tapping of the left glove
was patient at first,
like a spoon against the shell
of a boiled egg.
Then the slaps of the right glove,
spanking my face flush,
dizzy as the mambo record on the turntable,
my stomach a washing machine of nausea.
I saw my uncle smile.

Maybe this was his mouth smiling,
or maybe the punches' fever
conjuring the specter of a grin
in my spiraling brain.
But this was the moment
that I learned the lesson
of my uncle's nose:
cartilage squashed
by a gritted wincing swing.

THE YEAR I WAS DIAGNOSED
WITH A SACRILEGIOUS HEART

At twelve, I quit reciting
the Pledge of Allegiance,
could not salute the flag
in 1969, and I,
undecorated for grades or sports,
was never again anonymous in school.

A girl in homeroom
caught my delinquent hand
and pinned a salute
against my chest;
my cafeteria name was Commie,
though I too drank the milk
with presidential portraits on the carton;
but when the school assembly stood
for the flags and stiff soldiers' choreography
of the color guard,
and I stuck to my seat
like a back pocket snagged on coil,
the principal's office
quickly found my file.
A balding man in a brown suit
asked me if I understood compromise,
and we nodded in compromise,
a pair of Brooklyn wardheelers.

Next assembly, when the color guard
marched down the aisle,
stern-faced,
I stood with the rest,
then pivoted up the aisle,
the flags and me
brushing past each other
without apologies,
my unlaced sneakers
dragging out of the auditorium.

I pressed my spyglass eye
against the doors
for the Pledge:
no one saw my right hand
crumpled in a pocket
instead of spreading
across my sacrilegious heart.

Ceremony done, the flagpoles
pointed their eagle beaks at me,
and I ducked
under their drifting banner wings
back to my seat,

inoculated against staring,
my mind a room after school
where baseball cards
could be stacked by team
in a plastic locker.

THE OTHER ALAMO

—SAN ANTONIO, TEXAS, 1990

In the Crockett Hotel dining room,
a chalk-faced man in medaled uniform
growls a prayer
at the head of the veterans' table.
Throughout the map of this saint-hungry city,
hands strain for the touch of shrines,
genuflection before cannon and memorial plaque,
grasping the talisman of Bowie knife replica
at the souvenir shop, visitors
in white Biblical quote T-shirts.

The stones in the walls are smaller
than the fists of Texas martyrs;
their cavernous mouths could drink the canal to mud.
The Daughters of the Republic
print brochures dancing with Mexican demons,
Santa Anna's leg still hopping
to conjunto accordions.
The lawyers who conquered farmland
by scratching on parchment in an oil lamp haze,
the cotton growers who kept the time
of Mexican peasant lives dangling from their watch chains,
the vigilantes hooded like blind angels
hunting with torches for men the color of night,
gathering at church, the capitol, or the porch
for a century all said this: Alamo.

In 1949, three boys
in Air Force dress khaki
ignored the whites-only sign
at the diner by the bus station:
A soldier from Baltimore, who heard nigger sung here
more often than his name, but would not glance away;
another blond and solemn as his Tennessee
of whitewashed spires;
another from distant Puerto Rico, cap tipped at an angle
in a country where brown skin
could be boiled for the leather of a vigilante's wallet.

The waitress squinted a glare and refused their contamination,
the manager lost his crewcut politeness
and blustered about local customs,
the police, with surrounding faces,
jeered about tacos and señoritas
on the Mexican side of town.
"We're not leaving," they said,
and hunched at their stools
till the manager ordered the cook,
sweat-burnished black man unable to hide his grin,
to slide cheeseburgers on plates
across the counter.
"We're not hungry," they said,
and left a week's pay for the cook.

One was my father; his word for fury
is Texas.

This afternoon, the heat clouds the air like bothered gnats.
The lunch counter was wrecked for the dump years ago.
In the newspapers, a report of vandals
scarring the wooden doors
of the Alamo
in black streaks of fire.

AUTHOR'S NOTE:

WHEN SONGS BECOME WATER

CUANDO LOS CANTOS SE VUELVEN AGUA

In January 1991, I was honored to have several poems published in *Diario Latino*, an opposition newspaper in El Salvador. In February 1991, *Diario Latino* was burned down, on the behalf and at the behest of the same forces the newspaper had opposed: the government, the military, the death squads. The newspaper rebuilt itself, publishing only a few pages a day, till eventually *Diario Latino* was back to full strength. In February 1992, on the first anniversary of the fire, *Diario Latino* published the Spanish version of the following poem; in March 1992, the English version appeared in *Review: Latin American Literature and Arts*, no. 45. The poem was written in response to the fire and in tribute to the courage of the people who run this newspaper, though the poem applies as well to any people anywhere in the world whose voices rise above the flames.

—FOR *DIARIO LATINO,*
EL SALVADOR, 1991

Where dubbed commercials
sell the tobacco and alcohol
of a far winter metropolis,
where the lungs of night
cough artillery shots
into the ears of sleep,
where strikers with howls
stiff on their faces
and warnings pinned to their shirts
are harvested from garbage heaps,
where olive uniforms keep watch
over the plaza
from a nest of rifle eyes and sandbags,
where the government party
campaigns chanting through loudspeakers
that this country
will be the common grave of the reds,
there the newsprint of mutiny
is as medicine
on the fingertips,
and the beat of the press printing mutiny
is like the pounding of tortillas in the hands.

When the beat of the press
is like the pounding of tortillas,
and the newsprint is medicine
on the fingertips,

CUANDO LOS CANTOS
SE VUELVEN AGUA

—*PARA DIARIO LATINO,*
EL SALVADOR, 1991

Donde los anuncios doblados
venden el tabaco y el alcohol
de una metrópoli invernal lejana,
donde los pulmones de la noche
tosen tiros de artillería
en los oídos del sueño,
donde huelguistas con aúllos
tiesos en sus caras
y amenazas prendidas a sus camisas
son cosechados de los basureros,
donde uniformes verde olivo
vigilan la plaza
desde un nido de ojos-fusil y sacos de arena,
donde el partido del gobierno
hace campaña coreando por altavoces
que este país
será la tumba de los rojos,
allí la tinta de imprenta amotinada
es como medicina
sobre las yemas de los dedos,
y el compás de la imprenta imprimiendo motín
es como el torteo de la masa entre las manos.

Cuando el compás de la imprenta
es como el torteo de la masa,
y la tinta de imprenta es medicina
sobre las yemas de los dedos,

come the men with faces
wiped away by the hood,
who smother the mouth of witness night,
shaking the gasoline can across the floor,
then scattering in a dark orange eruption
of windows,
leaving the paper to wrinkle gray in the heat.

Where the faces wiped away by the hood
are known by the breath of gasoline
on their clothes,
and paper wrinkles gray as the skin
of incarcerated talkers,
another Army helicopter plunges from the sky
with blades burning
like the wings of a gargoyle,
the tortilla and medicine words
are smuggled in shawls,
the newspapers are hoarded
like bundles of letters from the missing,
the poems become songs
and the songs become water
streaming through the arteries
of the earth, where others at the well
will cool the sweat in their hair
and begin to think.

vienen los hombres con caras
borradas por la capucha,
que ahogan la boca de la noche testigo,
sacudiendo la lata de gasolina por el piso,
luego esparciéndose en una anaranjada erupción oscura
de ventanas,
dejando el papel para arrugarse gris en el calor.

Donde las caras borradas por la capucha
se conocen por el aliento de gasolina
en su ropa,
y el papel se arruga tan gris como la piel
de los habladores encarcelados,
otro helicóptero del ejército se desploma del cielo
con hélices quemándose
como las alas de una gárgola,
las palabras de tortilla y medicina
son contrabandeadas en rebozos,
los periódicos son acaparados
como bultos de cartas de los desaparecidos,
los poemas se vuelven cantos
y los cantos se vuelven agua
fluyendo por las arterias
de la tierra, donde otros alrededor del pozo
refrescarán el sudor de su pelo
y se pondrán a pensar.

—*TRANSLATION: CAMILO PÉREZ-BUSTILLO AND THE AUTHOR*

GLOSSARY OF SPANISH TERMS

Basora, José: Puerto Rican welterweight boxer who was famed for holding Sugar Ray Robinson to a draw in 1945, during the latter's prime.

bodega: neighborhood grocery store.

botánica: syncretic religious shop, specializing in spiritism and spiritual healing, full of herbs, potions, statues, books, etc., drawn from Catholic and West African beliefs fused in the Caribbean.

caciques: leaders of the indigenous people encountered by Columbus.

clave(s): in the singular, a two-measure rhythmic pattern, with three beats in the first and two in the second (though this is sometimes reversed), which forms the basis of the music called salsa and its Afro-Cuban antecedents; in the plural, a pair of wooden rhythm sticks that are used to play this rhythmic pattern.

Clemente, Roberto: Hall of Fame baseball player from Puerto Rico, who died in a 1972 plane crash off the coast of the island while delivering relief supplies to earthquake victims in Nicaragua.

coco frío: in Puerto Rico, a green coconut chilled, then cut open to drink the milk.

compañero: good friend; the word may also refer to a lover, or have connotations of political comradeship.

conjunto: literally, a musical group; here, a reference to Chicano folk music of South Texas, which features the accordion.

coquí: tiny frog, native to Puerto Rico, which sings at night.

Culebra: literally, a snake; here, a small inhabited island off the eastern coast of Puerto Rico, which was subjected to war games and target practice by the U.S. Navy for many years.

Diario Latino: literally, the *Latin Daily;* the major contemporary opposition newspaper in El Salvador.

Española: also spelled as Hispaniola; the name given by Columbus and the conquerors to the island now divided into the Dominican Republic and Haiti. Columbus was governor of the island from late 1493 to 1500.

Grito: literally, a cry or shout; the word has connotations of political uprising, i.e., the *Grito de Lares,* the Puerto Rican rebellion against Spain in 1868.

hidalgo: lesser Spanish nobility, many of whom followed Columbus to the New World.

Indio: Indian.

Isabela: the capital of Española, founded in late 1493 and abandoned a few years later; named for the Queen of Spain.

loca: crazy woman.

mambo: Cuban song and dance form, popular in the 1950s and 1960s.

marimba: a xylophone, indigenous to Central America.

piragua: literally, a canoe or small boat; in Puerto Rico, fruit syrup poured over shaved ice in a paper cup or cone, and customarily served from vending carts.

Santa Anna, Antonio López de: general who led the Mexican Army against the North American invasion of Texas in 1836, including the Battle of the Alamo; in 1838, he lost his leg in battle, and staged an elaborate funeral for the severed limb.

taxista: cabdriver.

tortilla: a thin pancake of corn or flour meal, customarily made by hand, which is a staple food of México and Central America.

Utuado: town in the mountains of Puerto Rico, where the author's father was born in 1930.

vida: life; the phrase "mi vida" (my life) sometimes serves as an expression of endearment, as here.

Vocero, El: literally, an advocate or spokesperson; here, a sensationalist newspaper in Puerto Rico.

BIOGRAPHICAL NOTE

Martín Espada was born in Brooklyn, New York, in 1957. He is the author of three previous books: *The Immigrant Iceboy's Bolero* (1982), *Trumpets from the Islands of Their Eviction* (1987), and *Rebellion Is the Circle of a Lover's Hands* (1990). His awards include two Fellowships from the National Endowment for the Arts, a Massachusetts Artists Fellowship, and the PEN/Revson Fellowship, as well as the Paterson Poetry Prize, for *Rebellion Is the Circle of a Lover's Hands*. Many of the poems in this volume arise from his work experiences, as a night desk clerk in a transient hotel, bindery worker in a printing plant, bouncer in a bar, welfare rights paralegal, and tenant lawyer, among others. Espada served for six years as supervisor of Su Clínica Legal, a legal services program for low-income tenants administered by Suffolk University Law School in Boston. In the fall of 1993, he became an assistant professor of English at the University of Massachusetts at Amherst.